I AM
COURTEOUS
ONLINE

RACHAEL MORLOCK

NEW YORK

Published in 2020 by The Rosen Publishing Group, Inc.
29 East 21st Street, New York, NY 10010

First Edition

Editor: Elizabeth Krajnik
Book Design: Reann Nye

Photo Credits: Cover Rido/Shutterstock.com; p. 5 Africa Studio/Shutterstock.com; pp. 7, 22 Syda Productions/Shutterstock.com; p. 9 Westend61/Getty Images; p. 11 praetorianphoto/E+/Getty Images; p. 13 Andrey_Popov/Shutterstock.com; p. 15 Beboopai/Shutterstock.com; p. 17 Astrakan Images/Cultura/Getty Images; p. 19 Chutima Chaochaiya/Shutterstock.com; p. 21 Budimir Jevtic/Shutterstock.com.

Cataloging-in-Publication Data

Names: Morlock, Rachael.
Title: I am courteous online / Rachael Morlock.
Description: New York : PowerKids Press, 2020. | Series: I am a good digital citizen | Includes glossary and index.
Identifiers: ISBN 9781538349564 (pbk.) | ISBN 9781538349588 (library bound) | ISBN 9781538349571 (6pack)
Subjects: LCSH: Online etiquette-Juvenile literature. | Internet-Moral and ethical aspects-Juvenile literature.| Internet and children-Juvenile literature.
Classification: LCC TK5105.878 M67 2020 | DDC 395.5-dc23

Manufactured in the United States of America

CPSIA Compliance Information: Batch #CSPK19. For Further Information contact Rosen Publishing, New York, New York at 1-800-237-9932.

CONTENTS

ONLINE COURTESY

Do you use the Internet to play games, do homework, or **communicate**? If you do, then you're part of the online world. You're a digital citizen! Knowing how to act online is an important **responsibility** for every digital citizen. You can be **courteous** online by using good manners.

5

NETIQUETTE

Rules about how to **behave** in real life are called etiquette. When you combine the Internet and etiquette, you get netiquette. Netiquette tells you how to act with courtesy and good manners online. It can help you make friends and treat people well. With netiquette, you can form strong **relationships** online.

7

THE GOLDEN RULE

Learning good netiquette can take time and practice. Luckily, there's one rule you probably already know. The "Golden Rule" says you should treat others as you'd like to be treated. Remember, the Internet is made up of real people around the world! They all have thoughts and feelings, too.

PLEASE AND THANK YOU

Whether you're online or offline, good manners often look the same. Saying "please" and "thank you" are simple ways to be courteous. It's also courteous to say hello and goodbye and to **introduce** yourself when you meet someone new. You can do those things online, too! Everything you type should be courteous.

FRIENDLY WORDS

When you're talking in person, your face and the sound of your voice give clues about what you mean. Messages online are different. It's important to think about how someone will read your words. Can your friends tell you're joking? Does your message make it seem like you're angry? Choose words that are friendly and kind.

13

CLEAR AND CORRECT

Before you post something online, be sure to ask yourself if your message is clear. Will others understand? Is your spelling correct? The way your words look matters, too. Have you seen messages written in all capital letters? It looks like the writer is shouting! Be sure to only use capitals in the right places.

THINK IT THROUGH

Things happen quickly online, but you should always think before you post. If you feel really sad or angry, that's a sign to slow down. Remember, everything on the Internet can be **permanent**. Your words and actions can hurt you and others. Slowing down gives you time to think or ask for help.

RESPECT OTHERS

Another way to be courteous is to show respect. You won't always agree with others. However, you should still respect everyone's right to share their ideas and beliefs. You can also respect others by respecting their **privacy**. If you find someone's digital **device**, don't take it or look at what's on it.

BE HELPFUL

How did you learn to use computing devices and the Internet? Your teachers, friends, and family members probably helped you. Now it's time to pass your knowledge along. Try sharing what you've learned about being courteous online with others, whether they're older or younger than you.

STRONG RELATIONSHIPS

Online courtesy and offline courtesy are alike. Having good netiquette starts with being courteous, kind, respectful, and helpful in person. Digital citizens know that the Internet is a powerful tool. It can help you build relationships. Being courteous online can help make those relationships stronger.

GLOSSARY

behave: To act properly.

communicate: To share knowledge or feelings.

courteous: Showing respect and thoughtfulness for others.

device: A tool used for a certain purpose.

introduce: To make someone known to someone else by name.

permanent: Lasting for a very long time or forever.

privacy: The state of being away from public attention.

relationship: The way in which two or more people or things are connected.

responsibility: The quality or state of being in charge of someone or something.

INDEX

WEBSITES

Due to the changing nature of Internet links, PowerKids Press has developed an online list of websites related to the subject of this book. This site is updated regularly. Please use this link to access the list: www.powerkidslinks.com/digcit/courteous